GAME BOY®
SECRET
CODES

////IIBRADYGAMES
TAKE YOUR GAME FURTHER™

GAME BOY®
SECRET CODES 2

LEGAL STUFF

Brady Publishing
An Imprint of Macmillan USA
201 West 103rd Street
Indianapolis, Indiana 46290

Game Boy is a registered trademark of Nintendo of America, Inc.

Please be advised that the ESRB rating icons, "EC", "K-A", "T", "M", and "AO" are copyrighted works and certification marks owned by the Interactive Digital Software Association and the Entertainment Software Rating Board and may only be used with their permission and authority. Under no circumstances may the rating icons be self-applied to any product that has not been rated by the ESRB. For information regarding whether a product has been rated by the ESRB, please call the ESRB at (212) 759-0700 or 1-800-771-3772. Please note that ESRB ratings only apply to the content of the game itself and do NOT apply to the content of the books.

ISBN: 0-7440-0057-2

Library of Congress Catalog No.: 00-93450

Printing Code: The rightmost double-digit number is the year of the book's printing; the rightmost single-digit number is the number of the book's printing. For example, 00-1 shows that the first printing of the book occurred in 2000.

03 02 01 00   4 3 2 1

Manufactured in the United States of America.

BRADYGAMES STAFF

Editor-In-Chief
H. Leigh Davis

Director of Publishing
David Waybright

Marketing Manager
Janet Eshenour

Creative Director
Robin Lasek

Licensing Assistant
Mike Degler

CREDITS

Title Manager
Tim Fitzpatrick

Screenshot Editor
Michael Owen

Book Designer
Kurt Owens

Cover Designer
Anne-Marie Deets

Production Designers
Jane Washburne
Tracy Wehmeyer

ACKNOWLEDGMENTS

BradyGAMES would like to thank everyone at
Nintendo of America, especially Cammy Budd,
Juana Tingdale, and the entire NOA Testing
Group. Your generous assistance made this
guide possible.

TABLE OF CONTENTS

TABLE OF CONTENTS

TABLE OF CONTENTS

GAME BOY® LEGEND

ABBREV.	WHAT IT MEANS
Left	Press Left on the + Control Pad
Right	Press Right on the + Control Pad
Down	Press Down on the + Control Pad
Up	Press Up on the + Control Pad
Start	Press the START button
Select	Press the SELECT button
A	Press the A Button
B	Press the B Button

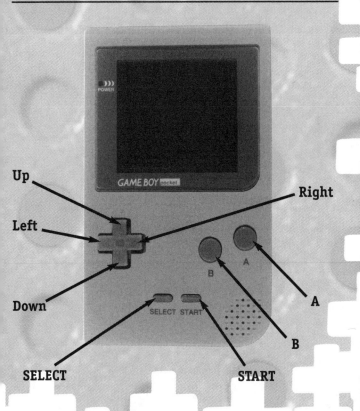

Up

Right

Left

Down

A

B

SELECT

START

A BUG'S LIFE

PASSWORDS

LEVEL	PASSWORD
1	9LKK
2	BL26
3	5P9K
4	6652
5	BKK2
6	2PLB
7	6562
8	L59B

Bonus	BL26

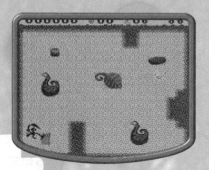

ALADDIN

LEVEL SKIP

Pause the game and press
A, B, B, A, A, B, B, A.

ANTZ

LEVEL PASSWORDS

LEVEL	PASSWORD
02	BCCB
03	DQGH
04	HGGF
05	NBFG
06	KGBF

A
B
C
D
E
F
G
H
I
J
K
L
M
N
O
P
Q
R
S
T
U
V
W
X
Y
Z

LEVEL	PASSWORD
07	QGJJ
08	GQHG
09	FLDP
10	KGQQ
11	DLGQ
12	CBHG
13	JBJG
14	PLDP
15	LFGB
16	DQLD
17	CLPG
18	DLHD
19	LFQG

GOOD PASSWORD

ARMORINES: PROJECT S.W.A.R.M.

UNLOCK THE CHEAT MENU
Enter the password BBBBBBBB to access the Cheat Mode.

ARMY MEN

PASSWORDS

LEVEL	PASSWORD
2	Grenade, Machine Gun, Helicopter, Jeep
3	Jeep, Helicopter, Helicopter, Jeep
4	Gun, Grenade, Gun, Grenade

ASTERIX: SEARCH FOR DOGMATIX

PASSWORDS

AREA	PASSWORD
Lutetia	CQPSJ
Massilia	MLSPS
Alexandria	RSFMS
Memphis	TPPGN

ASTEROIDS

CHEAT MENU

To enter the Cheat Menu, enter CHEATONX as your password, then press SELECT to enter the menu.

Level Select: Up or Down
Zone Select: Left or Right
The A Button toggles Invincibility

PASSWORDS

ZONE	PASSWORD
Zone 2	SPACEVAC
Zone 3	STARSBRN
Zone 4	WORMSIGN
Zone 5	INCOMING

A
B
C
D
E
F
G
H
I
J
K
L
M
N
O
P
Q
R
S
T
U
V
W
X
Y
Z

CLASSIC ASTEROIDS

Enter QRTREATR as your password for the original '70s version of the game.

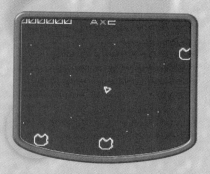

UNLOCK SECRET "EXCALIBUR" SPACESHIP

Enter PROJECTX as your password for the secret ship.

AUSTIN POWERS: OH, BEHAVE!

HIDDEN MESSAGES

Enter the FAB-DOS emulator and then enter one of the following words to see hidden messages.

SHAG
SHAGADELIC
HORNY
RANDY
BABY

AUSTIN POWERS: WELCOME TO MY UNDERGROUND LAIR!

HIDDEN MESSAGES

Enter the EVIL-DOS emulator and then enter one of the following words to view hidden messages.

EVIL
LASER
BIGGLESWORTH
MOJO

A
B
C
D
E
F
G
H
I
J
K
L
M
N
O
P
Q
R
S
T
U
V
W
X
Y
Z

AZURE DREAMS

CAPTURE RARE MONSTERS

Use an Ovaseed to capture Guardians and Souvenirs. Throw it at the monsters to catch them.

BABE AND FRIENDS

LEVEL PASSWORDS

LEVEL	PASSWORD
02	BOB
03	RN6
04	G5M
05	RM1
06	N6W
07	TYQ

BATMAN BEYOND: RETURN OF THE JOKER

LEVEL PASSWORDS

LEVEL	PASSWORD
2	C76564J
3	L88R8TC
4	Y539WZG
5	NTTJ9KY

BATMAN FOREVER

CHEAT MODE

At the Difficulty Select Screen, press **Up, Right, Down, Left, Up, Left, Down, Right**.

BATTLESHIP

PASSWORDS

STAGE	PASSWORD
2	QYBGTK
3	QYGZXK
4	GKPQZP
5	QRKGTD
6	QPDGYM
7	QQLGTD
8	QXFGTL
9	QNMGTK
10	NPGGYM
11	NXHGTL
12	NQBGYD
13	NQZGPD
14	NNCGYK
15	HJXQCN
16	NYDGTK
17	NWLGTM
18	NTFGTB
19	NRMGTD
20	BBQQBP
21	YPHGTM
22	YRBGTD
23	YRZGXD
24	YQCGTD

STAGE	PASSWORD
25	YSKGPC

26	BCSQBV
27	BDVQJQ
28	YYFGPK
29	BJRQZN
30	TRGGTD
31	JDNQJQ
32	TXBGTL
33	ZKTQKP
34	ZHPQCW
35	JCXQJV
36	TVDGTL
37	TTLGPB
38	JZWQKX
39	JMRQCQ
40	PXGGTL
41	CHNQBW
42	CGYQJS

A
B
C
D
E
F
G
H
I
J
K
L
M
N
O
P
Q
R
S
T
U
V
W
X
Y
Z

STAGE	PASSWORD
43	CDTQZQ
44	CBPQBP
45	CMXQCQ
46	CKSQJP
47	CLVQZV
48	PPFGYM
End	PQMGTD

BEAT MANIA 2: GOTCHA MIX

UNLOCK ALL SONGS
Enter the password: YEBISUSAMA

UNLOCK OTHER SONGS

Friends	MELODIOUS
Rydeen	GROOVY
Ultraman's Song	SUPERCOOL
Genom Screams	WONDERFUL
Unknown	SPLENDID

BEAT MANIA GB

EXTRA SONGS

Enter the following passwords for extra songs in Free Mode:

PASSWORD	SONGS
RELAXATION	Classic 3, E.N.K.
REMIX	Big Beat Mix
FEVER	Disco
SENSE	Disco, Big Beat Mix
VISUAL	Eurobeat, Big Beat Mix
MOTHER	E.N.K., Disco

D.J. BATTLE

Enter **BEATMANIA**, **KONAMI**, or **KCEK** to play DJ Battle on Free Mode.

BILLY BOB'S HUNTIN' 'N' FISHIN'

HUNT TURKEY AND PIKE

Enter the password: Pig, Boat, Bag, Deer, Bag, Deer.

BIONIC COMMANDO

FINAL BOSS

Enter the following password where S=Square, T=Triangle, B=Ball:

	A	B	C	D	E	F
1	S	B	S	S	B	B
2	T	S	_	T	S	B
3	T	S	B	_	T	B
4	B	T	_	B	B	T

RE-EQUIP

Hold **START** and press **A + B**.

BLACK BASS LURE FISHING

FISH BOTH LAKES

At the Password Screen, enter **K** in each space.

BLASTER MASTER: ENEMY BELOW

LEVEL SELECT CODES

LEVEL	CODE
1	E6C3D3KF
2	E6D3D3KG
3	E7C3D3KH
4	E7D3D3KI
5	F6C3D3KQ
6	F6D3D3KR
7	F7C3D3KU
8	F7D3D3KT

BOARDER ZONE

BONUS TRACK
Enter the password: 020971

LEVEL 4 & 5 TRICK ATTACK
Enter the password 290771. Levels 4 and 5 will now be available in Challenge Mode.

BOMBERMAN GB

ONE-PLAYER BATTLE MODE
Enter the password **5656**.

ATOMIC DETONATOR
Enter the password **5151**.

SOUND TEST
Enter the password **2145**.

ALL POWER-UPS
Enter the password **4622**.

PASSWORDS

LEVEL	PASSWORD
2	9634
3	1637
4	0320
5	6524
6	3260
7	4783
8	5472

BOMBERMAN MAX BLUE: CHAMPION

LOCATIONS OF CHARABOMS

Shell:	1-10
Pommy:	1-1
Seadran:	2-2
Panther Fang:	2-10
Beast Pommy:	3-3
Sea Balloon:	3-10
Puteladon:	4-4
Unicornos:	4-9
Iron Squid:	5-8
Animal Pommy:	5-15

CHARABOM COMBINATIONS

Aqua Dragon = Fire + Water
Pommy Dragon = Fire + Electric
Thunder Kong = Earth + Electric
Thunder Shark = Water + Electric
Rock Snakey = Water + Earth

BOMBERMAN MAX RED: CHALLENGER

CHARABOM LOCATIONS

Draco:	1-1
Elephan:	1-10
Marine Eel:	2-2
Knuckle Pommy:	2-10
Twin Dragon:	3-10
Big Ox:	3-3

CHARABOM LOCATIONS (CONTINUED)

Sharkin:	4-4
Hammer Pommy:	4-9
Iron Dragon:	5-8
Mecha Kong:	5-15

CHARABOM COMBINATIONS

Aqua Dragon = Fire + Water	
Pommy Dragon = Fire + Electric	
Thunder Kong = Earth + Electric	
Thunder Shark = Water + Electric	
Rock Snakey = Water + Earth	
Fire Force = Fire + Earth	

BUBBLE BOBBLE GBC

LEVEL PASSWORDS

LEVEL	PASSWORD
1	BBBB
2	CBCB
3	DBBD
4	FFBB
5	GGBB
6	HBHB
7	JBBJ
8	KKBB
9	LLBB
10	MBMB
11	NBBN
12	PPBB
13	QQBB
14	RBRB
15	SBBS
16	TTBB
17	CCBB
Boss	VVBB

LEVEL	PASSWORD
18	FCCC
19	FDBC
20	GFBC
21	JCCG
22	JBCH
23	LJCC
24	MCKC
25	NCCL
26	PMCC
27	QNCC
28	RCPC
29	SCCQ
30	TRCC
31	VSCC
32	WCTC
33	DBDB
34	XBXB
Boss	FCBD
35	GDBD
36	JCDF
37	KGCD
38	LHCD
39	MDJC
40	NCDK
41	PLCD
42	QMCD
43	RDNC
44	SCDP

A
B
C
D
E
F
G
H
I
J
K
L
M
N
O
P
Q
R
S
T
U
V
W
X
Y
Z

LEVEL	PASSWORD
45	TQCD
46	VRCD
47	WDSC
48	XCDT
49	GBCF
50	HFCC
51	JCFD
52	JBFF
53	KGBF
54	LHBF
55	MFJB
56	NBFK
57	PLBF
58	QMBF
59	RFNB
60	SBFP

BUBBLE BOBBLE JUNIOR

STAGE SELECT

Enter **Right Arrow, 5, Right Arrow, V** as your password. Press **START** to get to the Round Select screen. Press **Up** and **Down** to cycle through the rounds, and press **START** to begin.

BUGS BUNNY'S CRAZY CASTLE 3

PASSWORDS

LEVEL	PASSWORD
4	SXBX47
5	XCB84R
6	CTB84R
7	CSB8G7

A
B
C
D
E
F
G
H
I
J
K
L
M
N
O
P
Q
R
S
T
U
V
W
X
Y
Z

LEVEL	PASSWORD
8	TXB24H
9	1SB849
10	LCB8GW
11	5TBV4R
12	OLB84W
14	81BV47
15	45B2G7
16	GLBVG7
17	QLBVGW
18	?5BVGW
19	MDBX4K
20	30B84K
21	N0B8BB
22	28B8G2
23	R4B8G2
24	HGB24V
25	7MBXGZ
26	W3B8G6
27	JNBX4K
28	92B249
60	97X3GW

BUGS BUNNY CRAZY CASTLE 4

PASSWORDS

STAGE	PASSWORD
1-2	RHY043
1-3	HDY04?
1-4	7DY04Z
1-5	KQM04X
2-1	76504X
2-2	?GP04Z
2-3	TDP04X
2-4	KNYS4V
2-5	TQCS34
3-1	1DFS35
3-2	9DFS33
3-3	?Q5S34
4-1	T45S34
4-2	?XP83Z
4-3	RD5S3?
4-4	F4Y034
4-5	34Y032
5-1	WZY034
5-2	3GY030
5-3	WNP03Z
5-4	56303T
5-5	FZMJ24
6-1	5GM03T
6-2	W6WS3V
6-3	P6CS26

A
B
C
D
E
F
G
H
I
J
K
L
M
N
O
P
Q
R
S
T
U
V
W
X
Y
Z

STAGE	PASSWORD
7-1	PGCS22
7-2	FQMS24
7-3	M4PS27
7-4	WD5S20
7-5	3DPS22
7-6	H0F02?
8-1	70Y022
8-2	?8Y020
8-3	7SY020
8-4	HJP02Y
8-5	70P02Z
8-6	18P02Y
9-1	PSPJ15
9-2	H0FS17
9-3	72Y814
9-4	KSFS16
9-5	RSFS15
9-6	K0PS25
10-1	RJ5S11
10-2	1B3S1?
10-3	TB3S1Z
10-4	YLW011
10-5	PLW010
10-6	FBC01V
10-7	3BC01S
10-8	W2M01Z
11-1	POM01X
11-2	W53006
11-3	MSM01T
11-4	F0CS04

STAGE	PASSWORD
11-5	MJCSO4
11-6	WSW8OZ
11-7	38FSO2
11-8	F2M8OZ
12-1	PL3SO0
12-2	CSPSO5
12-3	5V3SO?
12-4	KQRO00
12-5	R6RJOT
12-6	1DTO01
12-7	TD900X
12-8	H4KJ?7
13-1	R4KJ?7

A
B
C
D
E
F
G
H
I
J
K
L
M
N
O
P
Q
R
S
T
U
V
W
X
Y
Z

BURAI FIGHTER

LEVEL PASSWORDS

LEVEL			PASSWORD
2	BRFG	NKMR	KDMT
3	KTDC	TCKP	SNNS
4	DRMF	NQTK	KMGT
5	SRSD	MQFH	MSKD

BUST-A-MOVE 4

EXTRA PUZZLES

At the Title Screen, press **A, Left, Right, Left, A**. A figure should appear in the lower right corner.

EXTRA CHARACTERS

At the Main Menu, press **Up, Down, Left, Left, Right, Up, A, B, B, A**.

38

BUST-A-MOVE MILLENNIUM EDITION

HIDDEN LEVELS
At the Main Menu, press B, LEFT, RIGHT, B.

BUZZ LIGHTYEAR OF STAR COMMAND

LEVEL PASSWORDS

LEVEL	PASSWORD
2	BBVBB
3	CVVBB
4	XBVBB
5	YVVBB
6	GBVBB
7	HVVBB
8	3BVBB
9	4VVBB
10	LBVBB
11	MVVBB
12	7BVBB
13	8VVBB

A
B
C
D
E
F
G
H
I
J
K
L
M
N
O
P
Q
R
S
T
U
V
W
X
Y
Z

CARMAGEDDON

UNLOCK ALL CARS AND TRUCKS
Enter the password: OZ6SZD[skull]V

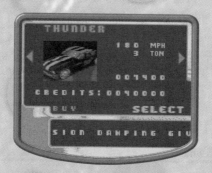

CHASE HQ

STAGE SELECT
At the Title Screen, hold **Down + A + B** and press **START**.

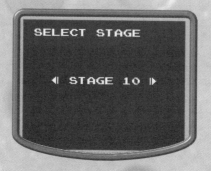

CONKER'S POCKET TALES

RESTORE HEALTH

Save the game when you're low on health. Then load your saved game. Your health should be full.

CROC

LEVEL SELECT

Enter the password: PQHPBFDHJB

DAFFY DUCK: THE MARVIN MISSIONS

PASSWORDS

STAGE	PASSWORD
2	72308
3	04070

4	82048

WEAPON SELECT

Defeat ten enemies, pause the game, and enter the following:

ITEM	CODE
Laser	Up, Up
Big Bullet	Down, Down
Bouncing	Left, Left
Rapid Fire	Right, Right
Health Refill	B, B
No Change	SELECT

DAVE MIRRA FREESTYLE BMX

FULL GAME

Enter the password: R6KZBS7L1CTQMH

DONKEY KONG LAND 3

INFINITE LIVES
At the Title Screen, press **Down, Down, Up, Left, Right**.

MATCHING CARD GAME
At the Title Screen, press **Up, Up, Down, Left, Right**. Press **START** to play the game.

DRAGON DANCE

LEVEL PASSWORDS

LEVEL	PASSWORD
1	3128
2	1497
3	7434
4	4136
5	9224

(CONITUED)

LEVEL	PASSWORD
6	6230
7	4592
8	7271
9	2315
10	2042
11	9913
12	9354
13	1720
14	3310
15	0170
16	5108
17	6482
18	1277
19	2460
20	4838

DRIVER

ACCESS THE CHEAT MENU

At the Main Menu screen, enter in the following code to unlock the Cheat Menu:
Highlight "Undercover" and press Up, Up, Down, Down, Up, Down, Up, Down, Up, Up, Down, Down. If you enter the code correctly, the Cheats Menu option will become available. Access the Cheats Menu and turn ON or OFF any of the options by pressing Right to activate them or pressing Left to deactivate them.

A
B
C
D
E
F
G
H
I
J
K
L
M
N
O
P
Q
R
S
T
U
V
W
X
Y
Z

DUKE NUKEM

LEVEL SELECT

At the "Press Start" screen, press Left, Right, Up, Up, Down, Up, Right, Left.

INVINCIBILITY

At the "Press Start" screen, press Up, Down, Down, Left, Right, Left, Up, Up. You should hear a noise if you enter the code correctly.

EARTHWORM JIM: MENACE 2 THE GALAXY

UNLOCK LEVEL 4

Enter the following passwords at the Password screen:

3bdnkg
3bbbbb
bb3hbl

ELEVATOR ACTION

"?" DOOR ITEMS

Enter a "?" Door with the following digits in the hundred spot on your score to get the item:

DIGIT	ITEM
1 or 2	Shotgun
3 or 4	Machinegun
5 or 6	Pistol
6 or 7	Grenade
8 or 9	Heart

EVEL KNIEVEL

UNLOCK SNAKE RIVER CANYON
Enter the password: LASTSTAGE

UNLOCK GRAND FINALE MODE
Enter the password: LEVELS

RESET YOUR GAME
Enter the password: RESET

FINAL FANTASY LEGEND

SOUND TEST
At the Title Screen, hold **Down** + **SELECT** + **A** for about five seconds.

FINAL FANTASY LEGEND II

SOUND TEST
At the Title Screen, hold **SELECT** + **B** + **START**.

A
B
C
D
E
F
G
H
I
J
K
L
M
N
O
P
Q
R
S
T
U
V
W
X
Y
Z

FROGGER

STOP TRAFFIC AND TURTLES.

Press **A, B, B, Left, Right, Up, B, A** during gameplay. If you do this properly, a traffic light should appear and stop all traffic, and turtles will no longer dive underwater.

GEX: ENTER THE GECKO

ALL REMOTES

Enter the following password by holding the indicated button and pressing the direction at each spot:

B + Down (x20), B + Up, A + Right, A + Left (x2), B + Down (x2), B + Right, A + Right

255 LIVES

To instantly max out your remaining lives, follow these steps:

A: When you have one remaining life, enter a stage with a bottomless pit.
B: Fall down the pit.
C: As the "fall over dead" animation is playing, exit the level through the Pause Menu.
D: Repeat steps A through C and you should have 255 lives. However, you will have to get a Red Remote from *another* stage to be able to receive a valid password.

GEX 3: DEEP POCKET GECKO

MYSTERY TV STATUS
Enter the password: 4BFBBBM329BBBBBBBB

GHOSTS 'N GOBLINS

LEVEL PASSWORDS

Quest 1

Level 2:	L Heart K Heart Heart Heart B L
Level 3:	Q Zero M Heart Heart Heart 1 H
Level 4:	P S 5 Heart 7 Heart B 4
Level 5:	T J R Heart 7 Heart 2 Heart
Level 6:	J J T Heart 7 Heart 7 L
Final Boss:	K D C Heart H Heart S H

Quest 2

Level 1:	G N Heart Heart K 0 0 H
Level 2:	G N 1 Heart 5 0 8 J
Level 3:	X 4 3 Heart 5 0 M R
Level 4:	L S 5 Heart 9 1 1 4
Level 5:	D N 7 Heart 9 3 Heart 7
Level 6:	X N 9 Heart 9 3 3 3
Final Boss:	N 8 C Heart K 4 0 N

A
B
C
D
E
F
G
H
I
J
K
L
M
N
O
P
Q
R
S
T
U
V
W
X
Y
Z

GODZILLA: THE SERIES

LEVEL PASSWORDS

LEVEL	PASSWORD
02	NCFRGJJBBK
03	DMTFLSBFQM
04	PKDJMPLNPS
05	KDQLHRNDCN
06	DQSPCFPFJR

GRAND THEFT AUTO

LEVEL SELECT
Name your character LEVELS or WENDY

HALLOWEEN RACER

ADVANCED LEVEL
To access the advanced level, enter the password 2!!MT9.

HARVEST MOON

FREE EGGS

To get free eggs, buy a chicken and, during the same year, take an egg after it has been laid. Hurl the egg against the wall; it will become stuck in the wall. Use your sickle to cut the egg from the wall and put it in a shipping box. Now cut another egg out the same way. You should be able to acquire nearly 100 eggs from a single egg in this fashion.

SELL EGGS AT CHICKEN RATES

Take an egg that one of your chickens has produced and put it into an incubator. Walk to the animal store with it and select "Sell Chicken," but highlight your incubating egg. The store owner will purchase the egg and pay the full price for an actual chicken.

HERCULES

PASSWORDS

LEVEL	PASSWORD
2	B7FG4
3	XTV5P
4	TV5DP
5	FX6NL
6	HGRSV
7	K7DGR
8	FTXCG
9	GSJ4H

CREDITS

Enter the password **CRDTS**.

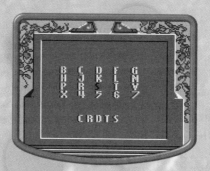

HOT WHEELS STUNT TRACK DRIVER

UNLOCK ALL CARS AND TRACKS

Enter the password: Down, Left, Up, A, Down, Right

LEVEL PASSWORDS FOR SHADOW JET

LEVEL	PASSWORD
2	Left, Up, Left, Down, Up, A
3	Right, Up, Right, Down, Up, A
4	Up, B, Up, Up, Left, A
5	B, Left, B, Up, Up, Left
6	Down, Left, Up, A, Up, Up
End	Down, Left, Up, A, Down, Right

LEVEL PASSWORDS FOR SLIDE OUT

LEVEL	PASSWORD
2	Down, A, Up, A, B, B
3	Left, B, Left, Right, Down, B
4	Down, B, B, B, Right, Down
5	A, A, Right, Right, B, Down

LEVEL	PASSWORD
6	Right, Up, Left, Up, Left, Right
End	Down, Left, Up, A, Down, Right

LEVEL PASSWORDS FOR TOE JAM

LEVEL	PASSWORD
2	B, B, Left, Up, A, B
3	Left, Left, Up, A, Right, Right
4	Left, Left, Up, Left, A, Left
5	Down, Up, Left, Down, Down, A
6	B, B, B, Right, Right, Up
End	Down, Left, Up, A, Down, Right

LEVEL PASSWORDS FOR TWIN MILL

LEVEL	PASSWORD
2	Down, Left, B, B, Right, B
3	Up, B, Down, Down, Right, Left
4	Right, Up, Right, B, B, Right
5	Right, Up, Right, Down, A, Right
6	Right, Left, Up, A, Up, Down
End	Down, Left, Up, A, Down, Right

A
B
C
D
E
F
G
H
I
J
K
L
M
N
O
P
Q
R
S
T
U
V
W
X
Y
Z

LEVEL PASSWORDS FOR WAY TOO FAST

LEVEL	PASSWORD
2	Right, A, Right, B, Left, Down
3	Down, Right, B, Right, Down, B
4	Right, Right, Down, A, Down, A
5	Up, A, A, Down, Left, Up
6	Left, Up, A, B, B, Right
End	Down, Left, Up, A, Down, Right

JAMES BOND 007

BONUS GAMES

Enter your name as one of the following:

NAME	GAME
BJACK	Black Jack

```
DEALER          BET+
                BET-
                DEAL
PLAYER

BET    $10
MONEY  $1000
 lack Jack    QUIT
```

BACCR	Baccarat
REDOG	Red Dog

JEREMY MCGRATH SUPERCROSS 2000

UNLOCK 250CC CLASS
Enter the password: SHJBBCGB

THE JUNGLE BOOK

LEVEL SELECT
Enter the password: BMHG

CHEAT MODE
During gameplay, press **SELECT** to access the Options. Select Music/Effects, and play the following sounds in order: **40, 30, 20, 19, 18, 17, 16, 15.**

KLAX

MINI GAME
Enter the password **Green Alien, Green Alien, Circle, Square.**

KONAMI GAME BOY COLLECTION VOL. 1

LEVEL SELECT FOR CONTRA
To unlock Level Select at the Title Screen, enter: Up, Up, Down, Down, Left, Right, Left, Right, B, A, B, A, START

A B C D E F G H I J K L M N O P Q R S T U V W X Y Z

THE LEGEND OF ZELDA: LINK'S AWAKENING

ALTERNATE MUSIC

Start a new player and enter your name as **ZELDA**.

SAVE YOUR MONEY

To save money on those big purchases, such as the Bow, carry an item to the counter, and as the money starts to drain, immediately press SELECT + START + A + B to go to the Save Menu. Select "Save and Quit," then reload your game. Depending on how fast you were, some or even most of your money should be left, and the game won't take what remains.

LOONEY TUNES: CARROT CRAZY

LEVEL PASSWORDS

Easy

01:	Treasure Island Marvin Martian, Elmer Fudd, Daffy Duck
02:	Crazy Town Daffy Duck, Taz, Elmer Fudd
04:	Space Station Yosemite Sam, Daffy Duck, Elmer Fudd

Hard

02:	Crazy Town Taz, Marvin Martian, Yosemite Sam
04:	Space Station Marvin Martian, Taz, Yosemite Sam

LUCKY LUKE

PASSWORDS

LEVEL	PASSWORD
1	Luke, Horse, Horse, Old Man, Luke
2	Coyote, Horse, Luke, Old Man, Old Man
3	Old Man, Coyote, Luke, Horse, Coyote
4	Coyote, Horse, Luke, Old Man, Coyote

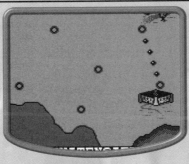

MARIO GOLF

EARN 300 EXPERIENCE

If you find the other three characters, you can earn 300 experience. You can't find the character you are playing as. Following are the locations of each character:

CHARACTER LOCATION

Sherry	Northernmost part of Tiny Tots
Azalea	Rightmost part of Palm's Putting Grounds
Joe	Leftmost part of Raven Woods
Kid	In the tree by the entrance to the Links Club Putting Range

LEFT-HANDED

Hold SELECT as you choose your character in order to play left-handed. This doesn't work with Sherry, Azalea, Joe, or Kid.

LEVEL UP MUSHROOMS

One is on the bookshelf in the room to the right of the director's room. The second is in the cabinet in the club maker's hut. Look in the bushes to the left of where you arrive at Peach's Castle for the third.

PEACH'S CASTLE COURSE

Win all four tournaments and beat each club's pro.

UNLOCK PUTS, GRACE, TINY, GENE YUSS

Speak to the character in the lounge that you wish to open up. Defeat him or her to play as that character.

UNLOCK WARIO

Defeat the club pros and tournaments.

MATCHBOX CATERPILLAR CONSTRUCTION ZONE

UNLOCK STAGE SELECT
Enter the password BG6S

MEGA MAN 5

PASSWORD
Enter the following password:

RRT_ _
ET_ _T
_E_RT
TTRRE
TRTRR

MEN IN BLACK: THE SERIES

FLY

Enter the password **0601**. This should give you an error. During the game, hold **SELECT + Up** to fly. Hold **SELECT + A** to get more firepower.

 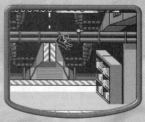

PASSWORDS

LEVEL	PASSWORD
2	2710
3	1807
4	0309
5	2705
6	3107
Ending	1943

Thanks Slick, but we need

STAGE SKIP

Enter the password **2409**. It should give you an error. While playing, pause the game and press **SELECT** to skip to the next level.

Aliens are on the rampage through the streets of Manhatt...

METAL GEAR SOLID

NEW OBJECTIVES

Complete the game on EASY to unlock new objectives for the original levels.

UNLOCK SOUND MODE

Beat all the VR missions: Time Attack and Practice Mode.

MONTEZUMA'S RETURN

UNLIMITED LIVES
Enter the password **ELEPHANT**.

UNLOCK ALL DOORS
Enter the password **SUNSHINE**.

FINAL BOSS
Enter the password **6JYBSPPJ**.

MR. NUTZ

LEVEL PASSWORDS

LEVEL	PASSWORD
2	DDMMNN
3	NNRRGG
4	CCLLRS
5	JJMPPR
6	SWWTCH

MEAN STREETS PART 1

MULAN

PASSWORDS

LEVEL	PASSWORD
2	JSFPW
3	QGHXB

NBA JAM TOURNAMENT EDITION

NO PENALTY FOR GOAL TENDING
On the "Tonight's Match Up" screen, press Right, Up, Down, Right, Down, Up.

EASIER INTERCEPTIONS
On the "Tonight's Match Up" screen, press Left, Left, Left, Left, A, Right.

EASIER THREE-POINTERS
On the "Tonight's Match Up" screen, press Up, Down, Left, Right, Left, Down, Up.

SLIPPERY COURT

On the "Tonight's Match Up" screen, press A, A, A, A, A, Right, Right, Right, Right, Right.

HIGH SHOTS

On the "Tonight's Match Up" screen, press Up, Down, Up, Down, Right, Up, A, A, A, A, Down.

DISPLAY SHOT PERCENTAGE

On the "Tonight's Match Up" screen, press Up, Up, Down, Down, B.

SUPER DUNKS

On the "Tonight's Match Up" screen, press Left, Right, A, B, B, A.

ALWAYS ON FIRE

On the "Tonight's Match Up" screen, press Down, Right, Right, B, A, Left.

NEW ADVENTURES OF MARY KATE AND ASHLEY

LEVEL PASSWORDS

LEVEL	PASSWORD
Volcano Mystery	CBTHPM
Haunted Camp	GMQTCK
Funhouse Mystery	LHDDQJ
Hotel Who-Done-It	MDGKMQ

NFL BLITZ

CHEAT CODES

Enter the following codes at the Match-Up Screen. The first number is how many times you press **START**. The second number is how many times you press **B**. The third number is how many times you press **A**. Then press the direction indicated at the end of the code.

CODE	EFFECT
2,0,2 Right	Brick Field
2,2,2 Right	Night Game
3,2,3 Down	Parking Lot
5,5,1 Up	Predator Mode
0,0,6 Up	Overtime
5,1,4 Up	Infinite Turbos

CODE	EFFECT
4,3,3 Up	Invisible Receiver
3,3,3 Left	No Pointer

4,2,3 Down	No Fumbles

PLAY AS EMERYSVILLE ECLIPSE
Enter the password **00606744**.

PLAY AS MIDWAY BLITZERS
Enter the password **06267545**.

ODDWORLD ADVENTURES

PASSWORDS

PASSWORD	DOORS OPEN
JCBCM	1
JCCCL	1,7
SCBCC	1,2
JDBCL	1,3
JFBCP	1,4
JHBCR	1,5

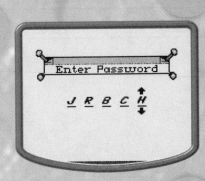

PASSWORD	DOORS OPEN
JMBCC	1,6
SCCCB	1,2,7
SDBCB	1,2,3
JDCCM	1,3,7
JFCCN	1,4,7
JMCCB	1,6,7
JHCCQ	1,5,7
JGBCN	1,3,4
JJBCQ	1,3,5
JNBCB	1,3,6
JKBCT	1,4,5
JPBCF	1,4,6
JRBCH	1,5,6

PASSWORD	DOORS OPEN
SHBCH	1,2,5
SFBCF	1,2,4
SMBCM	1,2,6
SDCCC	1,2,3,7
SFCCD	1,2,4,7
SHCCG	1,2,5,7
SMCCL	1,2,6,7
SGBCD	1,2,3,4
SJBCG	1,2,3,5
SNBCL	1,2,3,6
JRCCG	1,5,6,7
JPCCD	1,4,6,7

A
B
C
D
E
F
G
H
I
J
K
L
M
N
O
P
Q
R
S
T
U
V
W
X
Y
Z

PASSWORD	DOORS OPEN
JNCCC	1,3,6,7
JKCCS	1,4,5,7
JJCCR	1,3,5,7
JGCCP	1,3,4,7
JLBCS	1,3,4,5
JQBCD	1,3,4,6
JSBCG	1,3,5,6
JTBCK	1,4,5,6
SRBCR	1,2,5,6
SKBCK	1,2,4,5
SPBCP	1,2,4,6
SNCCM	1,2,3,6,7
SGCCF	1,2,3,4,7
SJCCH	1,2,3,5,7
SKCCJ	1,2,4,5,7
SPCCN	1,2,4,6,7
SRCCQ	1,2,5,6,7
SLBCJ	1,2,3,4,5
SQBCN	1,2,3,4,6

PASSWORD	DOORS OPEN
SSBCQ	1,2,3,5,6
JTCCJ	1,4,5,6,7
JSCCH	1,3,5,6,7
JQCCF	1,3,4,6,7
JLCCT	1,3,4,5,7
JBBCJ	1,3,4,5,6
STBCT	1,2,4,5,6
SSCCR	1,2,3,5,6,7
STCCS	1,2,4,5,6,7
SLCCK	1,2,3,4,5,7
SQCCP	1,2,3,4,6,7
SBBCS	1,2,3,4,5,6
JBCCK	1,3,4,5,6,7
SBCCT	all

A
B
C
D
E
F
G
H
I
J
K
L
M
N
O
P
Q
R
S
T
U
V
W
X
Y
Z

BIG DOOR PASSWORDS

PASSWORD	PART
TBCCS	2nd Part
TBHCN	3rd Part
TBRCD	4th Part
TBRDF	5th Part
TBTBT	6th Part

ODDWORLD INHABITANTS

LEVEL	PASSWORD
2-0	JCBCM
2-1	JMBCC
2-2	JMCCB
2-3	JPCCD
2-4	JTCCJ
2-5	STCCS
2-6	SBCCT
2-7	TBFCQ
3-1	TBKCL
3-2	TBTCB
3-3	TBTDC
3-4	TBTGF
End	TBTBT

A
B
C
D
E
F
G
H
I
J
K
L
M
N
O
P
Q
R
S
T
U
V
W
X
Y
Z

PAC MAN: SPECIAL COLOR EDITION

PASSWORDS

STAGE	PASSWORD
Stage 1:	STR
Stage 2:	HNM
Stage 3:	KST
Stage 4:	TRT
Stage 5:	MYX
Stage 6:	KHL
Stage 7:	RTS
Stage 8:	SKB
Stage 9:	HNT
Stage 10:	SRY
Stage 11:	YSK
Stage 12:	RCF
Stage 13:	HSM
Stage 14:	PWW
Stage 15:	MTN
Stage 16:	TKY
Stage 17:	RGH
Stage 18:	TNS

PASSWORDS (CONTINUED)

STAGE	PASSWORD
Stage 19:	YKM
Stage 20:	MWS
Stage 21:	KTY
Stage 22:	TYK
Stage 23:	SMM
Stage 24:	NFL
Stage 25:	SRT
Stage 26:	KKT
Stage 27:	MDD
Stage 28:	CWD
Stage 29:	DRC
Stage 30:	WHT
Stage 31:	FLT
Stage 32:	SKM
Stage 33:	QTN
Stage 34:	SMN
Stage 39:	THD
Stage 40:	RMN

A
B
C
D
E
F
G
H
I
J
K
L
M
N
O
P
Q
R
S
T
U
V
W
X
Y
Z

STAGE	PASSWORD
Stage 41:	CNK
Stage 42:	FRB
Stage 43:	MLR
Stage 44:	FRP
Stage 45:	SDB
Stage 46:	BQJ
Stage 47:	VSM
Stage 48:	RDY
Stage 49:	XLP
Stage 50:	WLC
Stage 51:	TMF
Stage 52:	QNS
Stage 53:	GWR
Stage 54:	PLT
Stage 55:	KRW
Stage 56:	HRC
Stage 57:	RPN
Stage 58:	CNT
Stage 59:	BTT

PASSWORDS (CONTINUED)

STAGE	PASSWORD
Stage 60:	TMR
Stage 61:	MNS
Stage 62:	SWD
Stage 63:	LDM
Stage 86:	DCR
Stage 97:	PNN

A
B
C
D
E
F
G
H
I
J
K
L
M
N
O
P
Q
R
S
T
U
V
W
X
Y
Z

PERFECT DARK

UNLOCK CHEATS IN N64 VERSION

Use your Game Boy version of Perfect Dark to unlock four cheats on your N64 version of Perfect Dark. Use a Transfer Pak and download your information from the Game Boy version to the N64 version. This will make four cheats available. You'll now have the Cloaking Device, Hurricane Fists, the R-Tracker, and every gun in Solo Mode on the N64 version of Perfect Dark!

POCAHONTAS

PASSWORDS

LEVEL	PASSWORD
2	KPGXH4T8
3	CMQZB6R1
4	JWDLF7K5
5	TGNDX3V9
6	HFSBD2M6
7	QZJRL1W4
8	BPXCV7Z3
9	SDLFT8G2
10	RWHJX9Z5
11	MVNGB4C6
12	KCQTD3W1
13	TBPRG5H8
14	QFCMX2B9
15	VDHKS6L7
16	BNJHZ1R9

POCKET BOMBERMAN

EVERY POWER-UP

To start the game with all power-ups, enter the code **4622**.

ALL ITEMS

Enter the password **5656**.

FIGHT ONLY BOSSES

Enter the password 9437 to play through boss stages back-to-back with all power-ups.

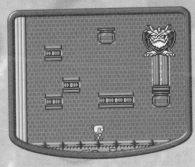

LEVEL PASSWORDS

Forest World

Area 1	7693
Area 2	3905
Area 3	2438
Area 4	8261
Boss	1893

Ocean World

Area 1	2805
Area 2	9271

Area 3 : Ocean

Area 3	1354
Area 4	4915
Boss	8649

Wind World

Area 1	0238
Area 2	5943
Area 3	6045
Area 4	2850
Boss	8146

Cloud World

Area 1	9156
Area 2	2715
Area 3	4707
Area 4	7046
Boss	0687

Evil World

Area 1	3725
Area 2	0157
Area 3	5826
Area 4	9587
Boss	3752

POWER QUEST

EASY 999,990
At the Password Screen, enter the password
1-R-7-5 F-L-V-D F-K-V-C.

ALL EQUIPMENT
At the Password Screen, enter the password
P-V-9-S 0-4-0-G 0-1-4-0.

```
-  PASSWORD  -

  P     V     9     S

  0     4     0     G

  0     1     4     0
                    ↑
```

PRINCE OF PERSIA

PASSWORDS

LEVEL	PASSWORD
2	06769075

3	28611065
4	92117015
5	87019105
6	46308135

LEVEL	PASSWORD
7	65903195
8	70914195
9	68813685
10	01414654
11	32710744
12	26614774
Jaffar	98119464
Ending	89012414

PUZZLE MASTER

PASSWORDS

LEVEL	PASSWORD
1	KING
2	FAIRY
3	WIZARD
4	MOUSE or CHAMPION

NOTE: Enter the word CHEAT as a password to have all of the tools right away.

PUZZLED

LEVEL SELECT

At the Password Screen, enter passwords EL001 through EL150, where the number in the code chooses a level between 1 and 150.

R-TYPE DX

DE SOUZA EDITOR

To unlock the De Souza Drawing Editor, you must beat R-Type, R-Type II, and R-Type DX. Then, at the Main Menu, press Right on the + Control Pad, and the De Souza Editor option should appear.

INVULNERABILITY

Beat the DX Game Mode on 10 credits or fewer, then in a non-DX game, press SELECT + A to become indestructible.

LEVEL SKIP

If you've already finished a stage, you can skip it by pressing B while the game is paused.

RAMPAGE: UNIVERSAL TOUR

PASSWORDS

SM14N1230	To play as George
S4VRS4560	To play as Lizzie

NOT3T3210	To play as Ralph

RAMPAGE WORLD TOUR

2-PLAYER LINK MODE

To open up linked simultaneous play, go to the Options Screen and hold SELECT, then press Up, Down, Left, Right, Down, Up.

RATS!

LEVEL	PASSWORD
2	WYH4TFGR9J
3	MMQ1DXXLT5
4	C7CDSFVRTQ
5	CW6F2FBLPG
6	LBBWQVDJJR
7	WRGSCD8QPN
8	BWBK8CBQQ4
9	4XLG-WJRD3
10	M1CS4YNKKW
11	5YMJFYJBC3
12	5TWKTYJCF7
13	CD588DDJ5L
14	BJR9XBLS4Q
15	5VLDPYJ8W?
16	WV4M3FRQKD
17	WDP6PDRM-N
18	VMF7YB9BND
19	BW7Z2CMKS8
20	VXXSTCRBD2
21	W8M-TF1MPX

A
B
C
D
E
F
G
H
I
J
K
L
M
N
O
P
Q
R
S
T
U
V
W
X
Y
Z

LEVEL	PASSWORD
22	CT3L4DWQ5B
23	MCVRJXPB7W
24	M12?BYFG7H
25	CXCPSFMJ3G
26	VD5H7BRQQ2
27	BWTTZCMM48
28	VWYMTC1NN?
29	V6D61B9SJN
30	BR5GGBMYSG
31	VW1TFC2GX-
32	4TRZ1VQDDK
33	5DYHMXZN5S
34	4Y4J1WZKJ3
35	M6R-DYBNMV
36	5BJDYXZSYS
37	WCY39D2T7P
38	L8NGVWBTJ5
39	MWH2VY4HF1
40	4JC-CVZPBT
41	L1CWSWVMJ5
42	BMJ2BBNTVG
43	M-?YSYBCYW

LEVEL	PASSWORD
44	W3NBFF2DPJ
45	VQ2C5BJYX7
46	4W1WRW9GXJ
47	B7S??CPKDM
48	C2FBZDPTT4
49	VT?6KC-BLN
50	4ZYT3VRC8X
51	VKLSTCTKNS
52	B4?LJBYCXV
53	W2VCKDTHPJ
54	MSXT4Y5DRB
55	43WCTVRT66
56	WWTK-DKB7-
57	L-1GZVWN?W
58	W9HN5D3CRX
59	M5DKJX5CKW
60	5QJ5FY179J
61	BGJ48CGCXQ
62	LB1?8WSC2M
63	LS84SW2CBG
64	57MWWX6R7X
65	MZ36JXJMM8
66	WXMLTDVNFD
67	WZ?MPD4NRJ

A
B
C
D
E
F
G
H
I
J
K
L
M
N
O
P
Q
R
S
T
U
V
W
X
Y
Z

LEVEL	PASSWORD
68	BVJDZBZQQG
69	4MZL1WDP86
70	CVNJGDZJW8
71	VNYVYCBSQJ
72	VDFDPCVRQS
73	V5SF1BBL6Y
74	MC256Y2K1H
75	CQFTZFQ75G

RAYMAN

ALL LEVELS PASSWORD
Enter CH5G4mSljD as a password.

ACCESS ALL LEVELS
Pause the game and press A, Left, A, Left, A, B, Right, B, Up, B, A, Left, A, Down, A.

FILL ENERGY
Pause the game and press B, Right, A, Up, B, Left, A, Down, B, Right.

99 LIVES
Pause the game and press A, Right, B, Up, A, Left, B, Down, A, Right, B, Up, A, Left, B.

READY 2 RUMBLE BOXING

FIGHT AS KEMO CLAW
Highlight Arcade Mode and press Left (x3), Right (x3), Left, Right, Left, Right.

FIGHT AS NAT DADDY
Unlock Kemo Claw, highlight Arcade Mode, and press Right (x3), Left (x3), Right, Left, Right, Left.

FIGHT AS DAMIEN BLACK
Unlock Nat Daddy, highlight Arcade Mode, and press Right, Left, Right (x2), Left (x2), Right (x3), Left (x3).

REVELATIONS: THE DEMON SLAYER

GET LOKI, PAZUZU, AND ASURA
Combine the following:

Suzaku + Kali = Asura (Asura has 1800 hp)

Zenon + Shiva = Pazuzu (Pazuzu has 1720 hp)

Zenon + Jinn = Loki (Loki has 1700 hp)

GET BAAL TO JOIN YOUR TEAM

First beat the game, then play the game again. This time, return to Mt. Palo and talk to Baal. He'll join your team.

GET LUCIFER TO JOIN YOUR TEAM

First beat the game, then play it again. This time, return to the Cave of Oasis. Talk to Lucifer and he will join your team.

A SECRET CAVE

In Luciferium, walk to the northwest corner. Find the hidden cave by exploring the mountainous region. In the Cave you'll find the Omega Armor, Omega Sword, the Alpha Mail, and the Alpha Sword.

GET VAERIAL TO JOIN YOUR TEAM

First Beat the Game. Then Return to the Nest of Zord. Talk to the Monster located on the Former Battleground.

ITEM COMBINATIONS

Lich + Harpy = Kelpie	L15
Mammoth + Kobold = Blue	L12
Blue + Kobold = Kelpie	L15
Kobold + Tanki = Kimalis	L8
Kobold + Kelpie = Larun	L13
Mammoth + Hecket = Kelpie	L15
Blue + Kelpie = Kelpie	L15
Mammoth + Hecket = Gayle	L10
Blue + Hecket = Lich	L1

A
B
C
D
E
F
G
H
I
J
K
L
M
N
O
P
Q
R
S
T
U
V
W
X
Y
Z

RUGRATS: THE MOVIE

PASSWORDS

LEVEL	PASSWORD
Train Crash	BVBYFJND

Hospital	TQMMY QK
Light Woods	RJDBCVRT
Dark Woods	VNGBLJCV
Ancient Ruin	LJTBWQQD
Reptar	BJGSMVSH

RUGRATS: TIME TRAVELERS

PASSWORDS

PVCJFJFR	Toy Palace North Wing
BVBYMJLK	Toy Palace East Wing
TPJCKLFS	Toy Palace South Wing

SAN FRANCISCO RUSH 2049

PASSWORDS

TRACK	PASSWORDS
2	MADTOWN
3	FATCITY
4	SFRISCO
5	GASWRKZ
6	SKYWAYZ
7	INDSTRL
8	NEOCHGO
9	RIPTIDE

A
B
C
D
E
F
G
H
I
J
K
L
M
N
O
P
Q
R
S
T
U
V
W
X
Y
Z

SKATE OR DIE: TOUR DE THRASH

PASSWORDS

LEVEL	PASSWORD
2	GNBF
3	MTGP
4	PVFS
5	FVCH
6	BXHN
7	GFTQ
8	JZWC

SMALL SOLDIERS

PASSWORDS

LEVEL	PASSWORD
4	Archer, Brick, Kip, Chip
5	Kip, Chip, Archer, Brick

THE SMURFS' NIGHTMARE

PASSWORDS

LEVEL	PASSWORD
2	Glasses, Pencil, Mouth
3	Soap Bubble, Mouth, Glasses

SPACE INVADERS

CLASSIC MODE
Enter the password CLSS1281999DBM

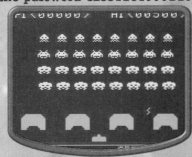

PASSWORDS

LEVEL	PASSWORD
1 Venus	RTJN PBKC X2RJPW
2 Earth	WWYX TC2N QW79VY
3 Mars	?WZ4 VCLN 4W81V?
4 Jupiter	RSSN 3QJ7 8?GJMC
5 Saturn	WSPZ MSO8 N?H8NF
6 Uranus	CV1? QWKG J3X8R5
7 Neptune	HV27 RW1G N3YOR7
8 Pluto	MV7H RCLH S3ZSR9

SPIDER-MAN

PASSWORDS

GAME LOCATION	PASSWORD
Venom defeated	GVCBF
Lizard defeated	QVCLF
Lab	G-FGN

SPY HUNTER/MOON PATROL

UNLIMITED AMMUNITION

At the Game Selection Screen, press Up, Down, Left, Right, Up, Down, Left, Right, Up, Left, Down, B.

UNLIMITED LIVES

At the Game Selection Screen, press Up, Down, Left, Right, Up, Down, Left, Right, Up, Left, Down, A.

SPY VS. SPY: OPERATION BOOBY TRAP

PASSWORDS

STAGE	PASSWORD
6	ZKP
11	YPT
16	MMD

STAR WARS: EPISODE 1 RACER

A FASTER ANAKIN

Collect every racer, and Anakin will be able to hit a maximum speed of 735 mph.

TURBO START

As the "1" fades from your screen, press the throttle button. If you get the timing right, you'll shoot forward ahead of the pack.

STREET FIGHTER ALPHA

INSTANT BISON

During any stage in the game, hold **A** + **B** + **SELECT** until the match starts. Bison will jump out and fight you instead of the regular character.

INSTANT AKUMA

When you're choosing between MANUAL or AUTO, choose by pressing both the A and B Buttons. Hold them down until your match starts. If you do this correctly, Akuma will jump out and fight you.

SUPER MARIO BROS. DX

YOU VS. BOO RACE LEVELS

Get 100,000 points in one "normal" game to access these head-to-head stages.

UNLOCK SMB FOR SUPER PLAYERS

Get 300,000 points in one "normal" game to unlock Super Mario Bros. for Super Players. This is the same as the Japanese SMB 2/Super Mario: The Lost Levels, except that Luigi is not available. Instead, Mario has Luigi's higher jumping abilities.

LEVEL SELECT

When you beat the game once, you can select your starting point.

YOSHI EGG FINDER IN CHALLENGE MODE

Once you've found at least one Yoshi Egg, a Yoshi option should appear in the Toy Box. Select it, and a random level's Egg location will be shown. At first, it only shows the screen you should find the egg on, but as you get more eggs, the hints become more detailed.

ALBUM PICTURES

To get all the album pictures, do the following:

Page 1:	(Top-Left) Fill up the Score Meter in Challenge
	(Top-Right) Get every medal in Challenge
	(Middle) Beat Original Mode
	(Bottom-Left) Beat all the Star Levels in Original
	(Bottom Right) Beat SMB for Super Players
Page 2:	(Top-Left) Get the end-of-level Fireworks
	(Top-Middle) Get a 1-Up Mushroom
	(Top-Right) Find and climb a Bonus Stage Vine
	(Middle-Left) Beat Original 1985 Mode
	(Middle) Save the Princess
	(Middle-Right) Use the link cable to trade High Scores
	(Bottom-Left) Get every Red Coin medal in Challenge
	(Bottom-Middle) Get every High Score medal in Challenge
	(Bottom-Right) Get every Yoshi Egg in Challenge
Page 3:	(Top-Left) Kill a Little Goomba
	(Top-Middle) Kill a Bloober
	(Top-Right) Kill Lakitu
	(Middle-Left) Kill a Cheep Cheep
	(Middle) Kill a Hammer Brother
	(Middle-Right) Kill a Bullet Bill
	(Bottom-Left) Kill a Koopa Troopa
	(Bottom-Middle) Kill a Spiny
	(Bottom-Right) Kill a Buzzy Beetle

A B C D E F G H I J K L M N O P Q R S T U V W X Y Z

SUPER MARIO LAND 2: 6 GOLDEN COINS

EASIER GAME

Press **SELECT** at the Pipe Screen.

PLAY THE DEMOS

DEMO	CODE
1	Up + SELECT
2	Up + A + SELECT
3	Up + B + SELECT
4	Up + A + B + SELECT

SURVIVAL KIDS

MINI GAMES

Fishing Game: Grab the big rock near the main river. Use the rock where you see fish.

Big Berry Game: First, get a monkey. Now, go to the big berry tree after the river. Use the monkey to play the game.

Egg Catcher Game: Go to the north of the desert with the monkey.

TARZAN

LEVEL PASSWORDS

The numbers in the Combos correspond to the symbols at the bottom left.

LEVEL	COMBO
2-1	4-2-3-4
3-1	1-1-5-6
4-1	2-3-7-4
5-1	7-7-3-1
6-1	6-5-4-7

TAZMANIAN DEVIL: MUNCHING MADNESS

LEVEL PASSWORDS
BLGNGJPDFFTJ   Unlocks China Level
LMBPBKTFKDPK   Unlocks Switzerland Level

TEST DRIVE 6

UNLOCK THE MEGA CUP
Win all of the other tournaments to unlock the Mega Cup.

UNLOCK CARS
Win the Mega Cup to unlock the BMW V12 LMR and the Panoz Roadster.

TETRIS DX

WALL-CRAWLING BLOCKS

A bug in Tetris DX allows you to push the "irregular" blocks (not 4-bars or squares) back up the wall. Hold Left or Right until the piece is pressing against the wall. Continue to hold the direction and quickly, repeatedly rotate the piece by pressing the A Button for the left wall and the B Button for the right wall. The block will "climb" up the wall slowly.

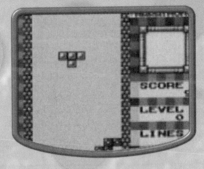

TOP GEAR POCKET

ALL CARS AND COURSES

Enter the password **YQXW_H**.

A
B
C
D
E
F
G
H
I
J
K
L
M
N
O
P
Q
R
S
T
U
V
W
X
Y
Z

ALL GOLD TROPHIES

Enter the password **YQX_%Z**.

NINE CARS AND SIX TRACKS

Enter the password **TWX+%Z** to get a head start that's not quite as big as the All Cars, Courses, and Trophies codes above.

TOY STORY 2

SCENE	PASSWORD
2	PBPP
3	BJWJ
4	PJBW
5	WBPP
7	JBPJ
9	JJWW
10	PBWJ
11	BPWW

End	WWWW

TUROK 3: SHADOW OF OBLIVION

UNLIMITED AMMUNITION
Enter ZXLCPMZ at the Password Screen.

UNLIMITED LIVES
Enter FJVHDCK at the Password Screen.

SKIP LEVEL
Enter XCDSDFS at the Password Screen.

EASY PASSWORDS

LEVEL	PASSWORD
2	SDFLMSF
3	DVLFDZM
4	VFDSGPD
5	CSDJKFD

A B C D E F G H I J K L M N O P Q R S T U V W X Y Z

MEDIUM PASSWORDS

LEVEL	PASSWORD
2	VLXCZVF
3	DPSDCVX
4	ZMGFSCM
5	HWKLFYS

HARD PASSWORDS

LEVEL	PASSWORD
2	CJSDPSF
3	CMSDKCD
4	SPFPWLD
5	TPDFQGB

TUROK: RAGE WARS

LEVEL	EASY	MEDIUM	HARD
2	K14QF4	3MQTL1	DT5JV1
3	3T5L31	Z1KMQ1	2F5QZM
4	SMJ54M	2TQCMR	MQ5LRS

V-RALLY
CHAMPIONSHIP EDITION

PASSWORDS IN ARCADE MODE

DIFFICULTY	PASSWORD
Medium	FAST
Hard	FOOD

WACKY RACES

ALL DRIVERS AND TRACKS
Enter MUTTLEY as a password.

WARIO LAND: SUPER MARIO LAND 3

DEBUG MODE

Pause the game and press **SELECT 16 times.** A box should appear on the lives. Hold **B** and press **Left or Right** to select a number to change. Press **Up or Down** to change the number.

WORMS: ARMAGEDDON

LEVEL	PASSWORD
Jungle	Pink Worm, Banana Bomb, Skeletal Worm, Pink Worm
Cheese	Pink Worm, Banana Bomb, Blue Worm, Dynamite
Medical	Skeletal Worm, Blue Worm, Banana Bomb, Banana Bomb
Desert	Red Worm, Pink Worm, Skeletal Worm, Blue Worm
Tools	Banana Bomb, Pink Worm, Pink Worm, Blue Worm
Egypt	Skeletal Worm, Pink Worm, Red Worm, Banana Worm

LEVEL	PASSWORD
Hell	Pink Worm, Blue Worm, Red Worm, Dynamite

LEVEL	PASSWORD
Tree-Hut	Red Worm, Skeletal Worm, Dynamite, Blue Worm
Garden	Banana Bomb, Red Worm, Skeletal Worm, Dynamite
Snow	Dynamite, Pink Worm, Blue Worm, Blue Worm
Constyrd	Pink Worm, Pink Worm, Banana Bomb, Banana Bomb
Pirate	Dynamite, Blue Worm, Dynamite, Skeletal Worm
Fruit	Skeletal Worm, Red Worm, Banana Bomb, Skeletal Worm
Alien	Dynamite, Blue Worm, Red Worm, Red Worm
Circuit	Red Worm, Dynamite, Dynamite, Dynamite
Medieval	Blue Worm, Dynamite, Skeletal Worm, Blue Worm

A
B
C
D
E
F
G
H
I
J
K
L
M
N
O
P
Q
R
S
T
U
V
W
X
Y
Z

WWF ATTITUDE

JARRETT PASSWORDS

OPPONENT	PASSWORD
Triple H	LGJCRMHG
Shamrock	PKHDSNJK
Val Venis	NJGFTPKJ
Steve Austin	RCFGLQBC
Gangrel	QBDHMRCB
The Rock	TFCJNSDF
Road Dogg	SDBKPTFD
Mankind	CRTLGBQR
Sable	BQSMHCRQ
Kane	FTRNJDST
Goldust	DSQPKFTS
X Pac	HMPQBGLM
Bossman	GLNRCHML

STONE COLD STEVE AUSTIN PASSWORDS

OPPONENT	PASSWORD
Gangrel	CBFPCQJC
Sable	BCDNBRKB
J Jarrett	FDCMFSGF
Undertaker	RQTKRBNR
Road Dogg	QRSJQCPQ
The Rock	TSRHTDLT
Bossman	STQGSFMS
Goldust	MLPFMGSM
Taka	LMNDLHTL
Al Snow	PNMCPJQP
Billy Gunn	NPLBNKRN

STONE COLD STEVE AUSTIN PASSWORDS
(CONTINUED)

OPPONENT	PASSWORD
Val Venis	HQKTHLDH
Edge	GRJSGMFG
X-Pac	KSHRKNBK

THE ROCK CAREER MODE PASSWORDS

VICTORIES	OPPONENT	PASSWORD
1	Road Dogg	GHKRCSCG
2	Taka	KJGSDRDK
3	Triple H	JKHPFRFJ
4	Bossman	CBDQGNGC
5	Godfather	BCFRHPHB
6	Shamrock	ZFDBSJLJF
7	Austin	DFCTKMKD
8	Edge	RQSBLJLR
9	Val Venis	QRTCMKMQ
10	Al Snow	TSQDNGNT
11	X-Pac	STRFPHPS
12	Billy Gunn	MLNGQDQM
15	Kane	NPMKTCTN
16	Mankind	HQJLBSBH
17	Goldust	GRKMCTCG
18	Gangrel	KSGNDQDK

A
B
C
D
E
F
G
H
I
J
K
L
M
N
O
P
Q
R
S
T
U
V
W
X
Y
Z

PASSWORDS

EDGE

RANK	PASSWORD
01	SHTPLMJG
02	BJQLPNHK
03	QKRMNPGJ
04	PBNSRQEC
05	NCPTQRDB
06	MDLQTSCF
07	LFMRSTDD
08	KQJDCBTR
09	JRKFBCSQ
10	HSGBEDRT
11	GTHCDFQS
12	FLDJHGPM
13	DMFKGHNL
14	CNBGKJMP
15	BPCHJKLM
16	TQSNMLKH
17	SRTPLMJG
18	RSQLPNHK

GANGREL

RANK	PASSWORD
01	TPSTPTHK
02	QLRQLQJG
03	RMQRMRKH
04	DSFDJDLN
05	FTDFKFMP
06	BQCBGBNL
07	CRBCHCPM

GANGREL (CONTINUED)

RANK	PASSWORD
08	JNKJDJQS
09	KPJKFKRT
10	GLHGBGSQ
11	HMGHCHTR
12	NJPNSNBD
13	PKNPTPCF
14	LGMLQLDB
15	MHLMRMFC
16	SDTSNSGJ
17	TFSTPTHK
18	QBRQLQJG

GODFATHER

RANK	PASSWORD
01	NGHNGDHG
02	MKJMKCJK
03	LJKLJBKJ
04	TCBTCKBC
05	SBCSBJCB
06	RFDRFHDF
07	QDFQDGFD
08	FRQFRPQR
09	DQRDQNRQ
10	CTSCTMST
11	BSTBSLTS
12	KMLKMTLM
13	JLMJLSML
14	HPNHPRNP
15	GNPGNQPN
16	PRGPHFGH
17	NQHNGDHG
18	MTJMKCJK

A
B
C
D
E
F
G
H
I
J
K
L
M
N
O
P
Q
R
S
T
U
V
W
X
Y
Z

PASSWORDS

KANE

RANK	PASSWORD
01	???
02	JBKBGRGG
03	GDHDKSKK
04	FHDHCLCC
05	DGFGBMBB
06	CKBKFNFF
07	BJCJDPDD
08	TMSMRGRR
09	SLTLQHQQ
10	RPQPTJTT
11	QNRNSKSS
12	PRNRMBMM
13	NQPQLCLL
14	MTLTPDPP
15	LSMSNFNN
16	KMJCHQHH
17	JLKBGRGG
18	HPGFKSKK

SABLE

RANK	PASSWORD
01	???
02	QCGMAKHG
03	TDKNSGJK
04	SFJPTHKJ
05	MGCQLDBC
06	NKDTPCFD
07	HLRBGSQP

SABLE (CONTINUED)

RANK	PASSWORD
08	GMQCHTRQ
09	JPSFKRTS
10	BRLHCPML
11	FSPJDLNP
12	DTNKFMPN
13	RLHLQJGH
14	FSNNFNQP
15	DTPPDPRN
16	RLGGRGDH
17	QMHHQHFG
18	TNJJTJBK

TAKA MICHINOKU

RANK	PASSWORD
01	DHJRMMGG
02	CJHSNNKK
03	BKGTPPJJ
04	KBFLQQCC
05	JCDMRRBB
06	HDCNSSFF
07	GFBPTTDD
08	PQTGBBRR
09	MRSHCCQQ
10	MSRJDDTT
11	LTQKFFSS
12	TLPBGGMM
13	SMNCHHLL
14	RNMDJJPP
15	QPLFKKNN
16	FQKQLLHH
17	DRJRMMGG
18	CSHSNNKK

A B C D E F G H I J K L M N O P Q R S T U V W X Y Z

THE UNDERTAKER

RANK	PASSWORD
01	SGKTCRHG
02	RKGQDSJK
03	QJHRFTKJ
04	PCDNGLBC
05	NBFPHMCB
06	MFBLJNDF
07	LDCMKPFD
08	KRSJLGQR
09	JQTKMHRQ
10	HTQGNJST
11	GSRHPKTS
12	FMNDQBLM
13	DLPFRCML
14	CPLBSDNP
15	BNMCTFPN
16	TRJSBQGH
17	SQKTCRHG
18	RTGQDSJK

X-PAC

RANK	PASSWORD
01	SCJPCHDG
02	RDHLDJFK
03	QFGMFKDJ
04	PGFSGBHC
05	NHDTHCGB
06	MJCQJDKF
07	LKBRKFJD
08	KLTDLQMR
09	HNRBNSPT

RANK	PASSWORD
10	GPQCTPNS
11	FQPJQLRM
12	DRNKRMOL
13	CSMGSNTP
14	BTLHATPS
15	TLKNBGCH
16	SMJPCHBG
17	RNHLDJFK

WWF WRESTLEMANIA 2000

BILLY GUNN

OPPONENT	PASSWORD
Road Dogg	PJH!
Val Venis	PJHT
Jeff Jarrett	PJKB
Shawn Michaels	PJM6
Big Boss Man	PJN9
Ken Shamrock	PJRW
The Big Show	PJSS
Shawn Michaels	PJWZ
Triple-H	PJXC
X-Pac/Ken Shamrock	PJZX
Steve Austin	PJ18
Undertaker	PJ3P
Kane	PJ59
The Rock	PJ7N
Mankind	PJ!C
Kane	PKBY
The Big Show	PKDY

A B C D E F G H I J K L M N O P Q R S T U V W X Y Z

STEVE AUSTIN

OPPONENT	PASSWORD
Ken Shamrock	CSD7
Jeff Jarrett	CSGQ
Road Dogg	CSK8
X-Pac	CSL3
Billy Gunn	CSP6
Val Venis	CSQS
Big Boss Man	CSTP
X-Pac	CSVW
Triple-H	CSX9
Shawn Michaels/ Val Venis	CSOT
Big Show	C525
Kane	CS4L
Mankind	CS66
The Rock	CS8K
The Undertaker	CS!9
Mankind	CTCV
Big Boss Man	CTFV

THE ROCK

OPPONENT	PASSWORD
Ken Shamrock	FSDM
Jeff Jarrett	FSH4
Road Dogg	FSKN
X-Pac	FSLH
Mr. Ass	FSPL
Val Venis	FSR6
Big Bossman	FSS3

THE ROCK (CONTINUED)

OPPONENT	PASSWORD
X-Pac	FSW9
Triple-H	FSXP
Shawn Michaels	FSZ7
Big Show	FS2K
Kane	FS30
Mankind	FS6L
Undertaker	FS7Z
Steve Austin	FS!P
Mankind	FTB8
Big Boss Man	TD8

UNDERTAKER

OPPONENT	PASSWORD
Val Venis	2BDM
Road Dogg	2BH4
X-Pac	2BKN
Billy Gunn	2BLH
Ken Shamrock	2BPL
Big Boss Man	2BRN
Shawn Michaels	2BS3
Billy Gunn	2BW9
Triple-H	2BKP
Kane	2B2K
The Big Show	2B30
Mankind	2B6L
The Rock	2B7Z
Steve Austin	2B!P
Mankind	2CB8
Shawn Michaels	2CD8

YODA STORIES

PASSWORDS

LEVEL	PASSWORD
2	XKJ
3	GJP
4	TDM
5	WTM
6	ZBV
7	QTC
8	TGR
9	VDP
10	BFG
11	FNP
12	STJ
13	FTG
14	BLP
15	YSF

GAME BOY® LEGAL STUFF

Game Boy® is a registered trademark of Nintendo of America, Inc.

A BUG'S LIFE ©1998 Disney. All rights reserved. ©1998 THQ, Inc. THQ is a registered trademark of THQ, Inc.

ALADDIN ©1993 The Walt Disney Company. ©1994 Virgin Interactive Entertainment. All rights reserved.

ANTZ ©1999. Infogrames. All Rights Reserved. "Antz" tm & ©1999. DreamWorks. All Rights Reserved

ARMORINES: PROJECT S.W.A.R.M. ©1999 Acclaim Entertainment, Inc.

ASTERIX: SEARCH FOR DOGMATIX

ASTEROIDS Developed by Syrox Developments Ltd. Published by Activision. All rights reserved.

AUSTIN POWERS: OH, BEHAVE!

AUSTIN POWERS: WELCOME TO MY UNDERGROUND LAIR!

AZURE DREAMS ©2000 Konami. Konami is a registered trademark of Konami Co., Ltd. All rights reserved.

BABE AND FRIENDS

BATMAN BEYOND: RETURN OF THE JOKER ©2000 KEMCO. Batman Beyond is the property of DC Comics. TM and ©1999 DC Comics. All rights reserved.

BATMAN FOREVER Batman and all related elements are property of DC Comics tm and ©1995. All rights reserved. ©1995 Acclaim Entertainment, Inc.

BATTLESHIP is a trademark and ©1992 Milton Bradley Co., a division of Hasbro Inc. ©1992 Use Corp. All Rights Reserved. Licensed by Mindscape, Inc.

BATTLE TANX™ ©2000 The 3DO Company. All Rights Reserved.

BEAT MANIA 2: GOTCHA MIX ©2000 Konami. Konami is a registered trademark of Konami Co., Ltd. All Rights Reserved.

BEAT MANIA GB ©1997, 1999 Konami. All rights reserved.

BILLY BOB'S HUNTIN' 'N' FISHIN' ©2000 Midway Home Entertainment Inc. All rights reserved.

BIONIC COMMANDO ©1992 Capcom. All rights reserved.

BLACK BASS © Starfish, Inc. All rights resreved.

BLASTER MASTER BOY ©1991 Aicom Co. Ltd. Reprogrammed game ©1991 Sunsoft. All rights reserved.

BLASTER MASTER: ENEMY BELOW Published by Sunsoft. All rights reserved.

BOARDER ZONE ™ & © 2000 Infogrames. Boarder Zone and Infogrames are trademarks or registered trademarks of Infogrames North America, Inc.

BOMBERMAN GB ©1998 HUDSON SOFT. Licensed to Nintendo. All rights reserved.

BOMBERMAN MAX BLUE CHAMPION/ RED CHALLENGER Developed by Hudson. Published by Vatical Entertainment. All rights reserved.

BUBBLE BOBBLE GBC ©2000 Taito Corp. All rights reserved.

BUBBLE BOBBLE JUNIOR ©1993 Taito. All rights resrved.

BUGS BUNNY CRAZY CASTLE 3 ©1999 KEMCO. Licensed by Nintendo. All rights reserved.

BURAI FIGHTER

BUST-A-MOVE 4 ©1999 Taito Corporation. All rights reserved.

BUST-A-MOVE MILLENIUM ©2000 Taito Corporation. All rights reserved.

BUZZ LIGHTYEAR OF STAR COMMAND ©Disney/Pixar. Activision is a registered trademark of Activision, Inc. ©2000 Activision, Inc. All rights reserved.

CARMEDGEDDON™ ©1999 SCi Ltd.
All Rights Reserved

CHASE HQ Published by Metro 3D.
All rights reserved.

CONKER'S POCKET TALES Developed by Rare.
Published by Nintendo. All rights reserved.

CROC ©2000 Argonaut Software Ltd.
All rights reserved.
Croc is a trademark of Argonaut Software Ltd.

DAFFY DUCK: THE MARVIN MISSIONS

DAVE MIRRA FREESTYLE BMX™ Developed
By Z-Axis. Acclaim ®, Dave Mirra Freestyle BMX™
and Acclaim Max Sports TM & ©2000 Acclaim
Entertainment, Inc. All Rights Reserved

DONKEY KONG LAND 3 ©1995-1997 Nintendo.
All rights reserved.

DRAGON DANCE ©2000 Crave Entertainment,
Inc. All rights reserved.

DRIVER ©2000 Infogrames Entertainment S.A.
All Rights Reserved.

DUKE NUKEM Developed by Torus Games.
Published by GT Interactive. All rights reserved.

**EARTHWORM JIM: MENACE 2 THE
GALAXY**
Developed by IMS. Published by Crave Entertainment.
All rights reserved.

ELEVATOR ACTION

EVEL KNIEVEL Developed by Tarantula Studios.
Published by Take 2 Interactive. All rights reserved.

FINAL FANTASY LEGEND ©1989 Square Soft.
Licensed by Nintendo. All rights reserved.

FINAL FANTASY LEGEND II ©1991 Square Co.,
Ltd. All rights reserved. Final Fantasy® and
Squaresoft® are registered trademarks of Square Co.,
Ltd. All rights reserved.

FROGGER is a trademark of Hasbro.
All rights reserved.

GEX: ENTER THE GECKO™ © Crystal Dynamics. All rights reserved. Published by Crave Entertainment. ©1998 Crave Entertainment.

GEX 3: DEEP POCKET GECKO Developed by IMS. Published by Eidos Interactive. All rights reserved.

GHOSTS 'N GOBLINS ©2000 Capcom Entertainment. All rights reserved.

GODZILLA: THE SERIES©2000 Crave Entertainment, Inc. All rights reserved.

GRAND THEFT AUTO Developed by Tarantula. Published by RockStar. All rights reserved.

HALLOWEEN RACER

HARVEST MOON Developed and published by Natsume. All rights reserved.

HERCULES ©1997 The Walt Disney Company. All rights reserved. ©1997 THQ Inc.

HOT WHEELS STUNT TRACK DRIVER

JAMES BOND 007 © Nintendo/Rare. ©1962, 1995 Danjaq, LLC. & U.A.C. All rights reserved. Game published and distributed by Nintendo. All rights reserved.

JEREMY MCGRATH SUPERCROSS 2000

THE JUNGLE BOOK

KLAX ©1990 Hudson Soft. ©Atari Games Corp. ©Tengen Inc. ©Tengen Ltd. All rights reserved.

KONAMI GAME BOY COLLECTION VOL. 1

THE LEGEND OF ZELDA: LINK'S AWAKENING ©1993, 1998 Nintendo. All rights reserved.

LOONEY TUNES: CARROT CRAZY © Infogrames. All rights reserved.

LOONEY TUNES: TWOUBLE © Infogrames. All rights reserved.

LUCKY LUKE Developed by Fernando Velez. Published by Infogrames. All rights reserved.

MARIO GOLF ©Nintendo. All rights reserved.

SKATE OR DIE: TOUR DE THRASH

SMALL SOLDIERS Published by THQ. All rights reserved.

THE SMURFS' NIGHTMARE

SPACE INVADERS

SPIDER-MAN Marvel Comics, Spider-Man: TM & ©2000 Marvel Characters, Inc. All rights reserved. Activision is a registered trademark of Activision, Inc. ©2000 Activision, Inc. All rights reserved.

SPY HUNTER/MOON PATROL ©2000 Midway Home Entertainment Inc. All rights reserved.

SPY VS. SPY: OPERATION BOOBY TRAP ©1992 Kemco. Published under license from First Star Software, Inc. Spy vs Spy is a registered trademark of E.C. Publications, Inc. ©1992 First Star Software, Inc.

STAR WARS: EPISODE 1 RACER ©2000 LucasArts Entertainment Company LLC. ©2000 Lucasfilm Ltd. All rights reserved.

STREET FIGHTER ALPHA ©2000 Capcom Entertainment. All rights reserved

SUPER MARIO BROS. DX ©Nintendo. All rights reserved.

SUPER MARIO LAND 2: 6 GOLDEN COINS ©1992 Nintendo. All rights reserved.

SURVIVAL KIDS Published by Konami. All rights reserved.

TARZAN © 1999 Edgar Rice Burroughs, Inc. and Disney Enterprises, Inc. All Rights Reserved.

TAZMANIAN DEVIL: MUNCHING MADNESS ©2000 SUNSOFT. SUNSOFT is a registered trademark of Sun Corporation of America. Loony Tunes characters, names, and all related indicia are trademarks of Warner Bros.

TEST DRIVE 6 Test Drive and Infogrames are the trademarks or registered trademarks of Infogrames North America. Test Drive 6, ©1999 Infogrames North America. All rights reserved.

TETRIS DX ©Nintendo. All rights reserved.

TOP GEAR POCKET Developed by Vision Works. Published by Kemco. All rights reserved.

TOY STORY 2 ©Disney/Pixar. Original Toy Story elements ©Disney. All rights reserved. Mr. Potato Head® and Mrs. Potato Head® are registered trademarks of Hasbro, Inc. Used with permission. ©Hasbro, Inc. All rights reserved. Slinky® Dog ©James Inc.

TUROK 3: SHADOW OF OBLIVION

TUROK: RAGE WARS ©1999 Acclaim Entertainment, Inc. All rights reserved. Turok ® and © GBPC, INC. All rights reserved.

V-RALLY CHAMPIONSHIP EDITION ©1999 Infogrames All rights reserved.

WACKY RACES ©2000 Infogrames Entertainment S.A.. All rights reserved. DASTARDLY & MUTTLEY AND THE WACKY RACES and all related characters and elements are trademarks of Hanna-Barbera. ©2000 Hanna-Barbera and Heatter-Quigley.

WARIO LAND: SUPER MARIO LAND 3 ©1993 Nintendo. All rights reserved.

WORMS: ARMAGEDDON ©2000 Infogrames Entertainment S.A.. All rights reserved.

WWF ATTITUDE ©1999 Titan Sports, Inc. All rights reserved. GAME CODE ©1999 Acclaim Entertainment, Inc.

WWF WRESTLEMANIA 2000 ©2000 THQ Inc. ©2000 Titan Sports, Inc. WWF™ ©2000 Titan Sports. All rights reserved.

YODA STORIES ©2000 THQ Inc. ©2000 LucasArts Entertainment Company LLC. ©2000 Lucasfilm Ltd. All rights reserved.